SU

SECRETS OF OUR

ANCESTORS

Survive Any "End of the World as We Know it" Disaster with these Long LOST Survival Secrets

INTRODUCTION

In this book, you will find a detailed account of the forgotten skills of our ancestors that need to be relearned to survive an 'end of the world as we know it's a crisis. These skills were practiced by the pioneers and farmers who migrated across America in the 1700s and 1800s and native American tribes.

Moreover, it involves the skills employed by our grandparents and great-grandparents to survive the Great Depression. These people were truly hard-working; they knew how to make use of what they had. These are the people that have faced some of the darkest times in the history of the US. Therefore, it is very important to learn from them.

For this book, we have divided these skills into the following 9 categories:

- Shelter
- Food
- Water
- Hygiene
- Medicine
- Transportation
- Safety and defense
- Trade
- Other skills

All the skills you see above are listed in order of their importance. It is very important to keep in mind that shelter is the top survival element. You simply cannot survive without a good shelter; what good are food and water and all other skills going to be if you simply die from a lack of shelter. This still does not mean that other skills are not essential to your survival; they are also necessary.

Gathering food and water will require more consistent efforts as compared to other survival skills. Also, a great thing about this book is that this book does not only give detailed independent information for all the skills. You will notice that there is a strong link between all the skills; everything is interconnected. We have even discussed the complications that can arise in practicing each skill and how to deal with them.

Moreover, we have explained the safety precautions for practicing all the skills in great detail. There are no gaps. We want to provide you with a full set of survival knowledge. Even if you do not take the possibility of an end of the world event seriously and you're here just out of curiosity, you will realize by the end of this book just how important it is to learn these survival skills of our ancestors.

Except for these essential skills, we have also listed other skills that will help you not only survive but begin to get comfortable in your new reality. It is obvious that to live a good life; you need to have a good psychological state. We have talked about ways to kill time and have fun, deal with anxiety and build good community fellowship.

The most important skills are explained in great detail. Step-by-step procedures are explained where needed. Moreover, all the necessary equipment to make use of these skills are also listed out. This book is like a one-stop shop; you do not have to go anywhere else. You do not have to wander on the internet and look at all these skills individually and end up confusing yourself even more.

SHELTER

You might think that food or water is the most important thing for surviving a crisis. But you're wrong! The shelter should be your number one survival priority. You simply cannot survive if you don't have shelter. The shelter will help maintain your body at its proper temperature and protect you from harmful elements, insects, and animals around you. What good are food and water going to be if you can't even protect yourself? Therefore, knowing how to build a shelter is super important.

Now, when it comes to building a shelter, you have to follow these three simple steps.

1. Choose your site: When considering a particular site to build shelter, make sure it is dry and flat. It should not be right next to a body of water or underneath any cliffs or falling rocks. Make sure it has a good fireplace near the front of the doorway.
2. Assess your needs: A shelter should be designed to serve your needs.
3. Decide on the type of shelter: This is the most critical part as many shelters serve different purposes.

TYPES OF SHELTERS

- Round lodge: A round lodge can protect you from extreme wind, rain, cold, and sun. It is similar in structure to a tipi, with an additional solid doorway. You can cover it with grass or mats or with a thick coat of leaf litter.
- Ramada: Ramada is a shelter that provides shade in hot, sunny weather. However, its flat roof doesn't exactly give you leak-proof rain protection. Ramada has many variations, but most have four posts, lightweight beams, and a good roof covering.
- Quinzhee: The quinzhee is a snow shelter similar to an igloo but relatively easy to construct. Snow must be just enough to construct an igloo. Most

types of snowfall can be used easily for constructing quinzhee. Pile up some moveable gear under a tarp to make a quinzhee.

- Snow cave: This is a very dangerous shelter to create, as it puts inhabitants at risk of suffering from low oxygen or even being buried alive in case of the ceiling collapse. You'll need a deep, solid snow bank or drift to build it.
- Wedge tarp: This tarp shelter is most suitable for windy situations with a constant prevailing wind direction. The wedge gives an aerodynamic shape to the shelter, which can resist the strongest winds and rain.
- Tarp wing: This type of tarp configuration is very effective for rain protection over a smaller area, but it can cover a bigger area when using bigger tarps.
- Tarp burrito: The tarp burrito is a low drag shelter with zero frills and can be set up in a 30-second window. Place your tarp simply in a likely shelter location. Fold it like a burrito.
- Tarp tipi: You only need a bit of rope, poles, and a tarp to construct one of the most unique and mobile shelters.
- A-Frame tarp shelter: The A-frame is a tarp design that provides good protection against rain and wind, especially when built close to the ground. When suspended higher, it still protects from rain but allows more airflow beneath.
- Desert tarp: To build this shelter, two tarps and several dozen feet of rope are required. Put one of your tarps out over the low spot and take each of the stakes at a corner of the tarp. Make sure you tie the tarps with stakes tightly and then tie the other tarp into place – so that there is at least one foot of air space between the two tarps.
- Tarp hammock: It is easy to improvise a hammock to get off the ground in wet or potentially bug-infested environments. An 8×10 tarp and ¼ inch braided nylon rope should be used.
- Wicki-up: The wicki-up is similar to a small tipi built using poles, brush, and vegetation. Thicker brush, grass, and leaf coverings on the steeper roof can protect from occasional rain.
- Leaf hut: The leaf hut is a two-sided, wedge-shaped shelter with effective weatherproofing and insulating properties. A long, sturdy pole nine to12 feet long is perfect for making a leaf hut.
- Lean-To: It is a basic, one-sided design that protects you from extreme wind and rain that the wilderness might throw at you.

15 HOME MAINTENANCE TASKS EVERY HOMEOWNER SHOULD KNOW HOW TO DO

You won't survive life after an end-of-the-world event if you do not even have basic home maintenance skills. Imagine you are the sole survivor after such an event, and you don't even have the basic skills to take care of your house.

You will probably have a lot of trouble trying to survive. Even if you are living a normal life, such skills will help you save money.

However, be careful before you start trying to fix everything on your own. You could result in extra damage to your home and yourself. Therefore, you should learn the below-mentioned skills as soon as possible.

1) Cut off the main water supply

2) Unclog a sink or drain

3) Clean front-load washers and dryers

4) Re-caulk

5) Clean the garbage disposal

6) Clean the dishwasher

7) Clean gutters and downspouts

8) Install household weatherproofing

9) Fix sticky drawers

10) Replace air filters

11) Patch a hole in the wall

12) Replace a light fixture

13) Pressure wash

14) Replace a window screen

15) Replace outlet covers

KEEPING WARM

One of your biggest challenges to survive on your own will be to deal with extreme temperatures. If you find yourself in a cold region without knowing how to keep yourself warm, you can die from the cold. You certainly don't want that, neither do we. So, let's take a look at how to keep yourself warm.

How to Build a Fire Without Matches

1. Friction-based
    - The hand drill
        - Make a tinder nest
        - Cut a V-shaped notch
        - Place the bark underneath the notch
        - Start spinning
        - Blow gently on the nest
    - Fire plough
        - Prepare the fireboard
        - Rub spindle against the fireboard
        - Blow on to the nest as you catch an ember
    - Blow drill
        - Find a socket and make a bow
        - Prepare the fireboard
        - String up the spindle
        - Start sawing
        - Blow on the nest as you catch an ember
    - Flint and steel

- Strike the steel against flint repeatedly
- Fold up your char cloth around the tinder nest and gently blow on it to start a flame to ignite the fire.
2. Lens-based methods
   - Traditional lenses
     - Face the lens towards the sun to focus the beam into a tiny area. Place the tinder nest under this spot, and you'll soon have ignited the fire.
   - Balloons and condoms
     - Condoms and balloons have a shorter focal length than ordinary lenses. To make fire, fill them with water and hold them 1 to 2 inches above the tinder.
   - Fire from ice
     - Shape the ice into a lens with a knife. Aim the ice lens at the sun
   - Soda can and chocolate bar
     - Rub the bottom of the soda can come with chocolate. Sunlight reflects off the polished bottom. Angle it towards the sun.
   - Batteries and steel wool
     - Stretch out the wool and rub the battery on it. The wool will begin burning.

How to Warm a House Without Electricity

In a crisis, it can potentially be very important to produce heat without electricity, insulate against heat loss, and keep your body temperature stable when the weather is a bit extreme.

- Find yourself a Wood Cook Stove or Pot Belly Stove
- Set Up an Outdoor Wood Furnace
- Buy a Generator (diesel-powered or gas powered)
- Get Propane Heater
- Make a Flowerpot Heater
- Solar Heat (Passive and active)
- Dress in Layers (Base Layer, Insulating Layer, Waterproof Shell)
- Insulate Windows

Lighting Without Power

Candle making

From a survivalist perspective, making candles on your own and stocking them up can be very helpful. Even though candle-making can be very useful and enjoyable, don't forget your safety while making them. After all, wax is a dangerous fuel. You will be surprised to know that ingredients used to make paraffin wax are the same ingredients used in making rocket fuel.

- Hand-Dipped Candles
    - Cover the surfaces and the floor with a newspaper or tarp
    - Put wax in a wax melter and heat it
    - Tie three to four wicks of wax to a wooden spoon
    - Dip the wicks in the melted wax, leaving one inch on the top.
    - Use a sharp knife to cut the bottoms for a flat surface.
- Rolled Honeycomb Candles
    - Push the wick into one edge of the wax, leaving 1 inch above the wax. Slowly, roll the wax-up tightly and evenly
    - After this, use your hand to smoothen the raw edge to blend it into the candle. Store honeycomb candles in cool and dry places
- Milk Carton Candles
    - Wash an empty paper milk carton and dry it
    - Melt candle wax using a wax melter
    - Cut a wick that is three to four inches bigger than a milk carton.
    - Pour the wax into the milk carton until it gets full. Leave it to harden completely.

How to Make a Torch

Making a torch using simple materials is the perfect way to bring light whenever needed. You might not think it is important right now, but it will be essential for surviving in crisis times.

Torches are improvised from sticks of wood (or branches), preferably wet/greenwood, as it prevents the fire from burning it up. You can also use river canes, cattails, reeds, and bark. The simplest torch design is a stick featuring a bundle of rags bound to one end soaked in tree sap, pitch, oil, or animal fat. If rags are unavailable, you can also use bark around the stick's end and bury it in dry grass, moss, small bits of wood, or leaves around it.This simple survival torch can last for hours.

FOOD

The importance of eating food is quite obvious. It fuels our body. We cannot survive without the nutrients that come from food. So, if you were to find yourself in an end-of-the-world situation, knowing how to get yourself food will be essential to your survival.

In this chapter, we will look at how to raise, hunt, and butcher animals. We'll also learn a bit about gardening. And much more!

RAISING ANIMALS/LIVESTOCK

Raising your animal is a great way to get yourself healthy food. But you can't just raise any animals; you need healthy animals for you and are easy to raise.

What types of animals to raise?

- Chickens: Poultry takes very little effort as compared to other animals. That's about it! Collect eggs daily, keep the coop closed off from predators, don't let your chicken catch diseases like worms, lice, and mites.
- Goats: You can get meat, milk, and fleece from goats. Goats love grazing and are good at keeping the weeds away. But keep an eye on them as they can escape easily.
- Sheep: They graze very well and provide wool, lambs, meat, and milk. Just like goats, they can escape easily, too, so keep them in fences.
- Rabbits: They are quiet, easy to handle, good for meat production, and cheap. Rabbits should be kept in dry places and need protection from high temperatures and predators.

- Pigs: The great thing about pigs is that they eat about anything and fatten up easily. However, if not kept properly, they can wreck good grass. Also, be mindful of them catching diseases like mastitis after farrowing.

How to store and care for them

Fence building

There are countless fencing options available. You have to understand your requirements. Consider your budget and the kind of animals you want to raise. Once you have a clear idea of what you should install, you can now choose the right option for you. Some of the fence post options are:

- Metal T-post fence
- Treated wood fence
- Locust fence
- Step-in fence
- Welded wire fence
- Woven wire fence
- Field fence wire
- Barbed wire fence

LIVESTOCK SHELTERS/BARNS

You will need different types of specific buildings to shelter your livestock. Most shelters have a main barn and multiple outbuildings. You must fully enclose livestock barns and shelter as they provide warm, dry shelter during bad weather.

Moreover, chickens need specialized housing. Hen houses have nesting boxes for laying eggs. Chicken coops are a type of shelter that has an indoor area for nighttime. It protects chickens from predators. There are many types of livestock shelters available there; you can even customize them according to your needs.

HUNTING

What to hunt

Being able to hunt animals is going to be a skill essential to your survival. There are many animals out there in the wilderness, but not all animals are healthy for you. Therefore, you need to have complete knowledge of healthy animals that can be hunted easily. Here are a few:

- Dove: Doves can be found easily all over the US and are very easy to handle.
- Rabbit: Rabbits are very nutritious and contain almost no fat.
- Groundhog: It is a type of ground squirrel.
- Deer: It tastes similar to beef and has very little fat.
- Wild turkey: It tastes very good, but it's hard to hunt.
- Wild boar/pig: Older boars have a musky flavor.

Bow hunting

Bow hunting is a simple yet elegant way of hunting animals. It has been used for more than thousands of years. If you find yourself in a perilous situation without any hunting tools, you will need to build a bow and arrow from scratch. Here's how to build it:

1. Choose strong yet flexible material for the bow and arrow
2. Use charcoal to put markers
3. Carve the bow into shape with a knife
4. Make a notch on the sides of the tip of the bow
5. Cook pine sap to turn it into the glue and use it to attach the arrowhead to the arrow shaft

Spear hunting

Hunting with a spear is one of the oldest methods of hunting in the world. To successfully hunt with the spear, you must have good technique. You must patiently stalk and then hunt the animal at the right time. Following, tracking, and finding the animal is very important. You need to be able to move quietly without alerting your target.

FISHING

10 ways to catch fish without a fishing pole

Fishing can also be essential to your survival if you are stranded next to a body of water. You should be able to catch fish without a fishing pole; here are a few ways:

1. Hand fishing
2. Gillnet
3. Dip net
4. Fish spear
5. Fish poison
6. Hook and line
7. Gorge hooks
8. Striking iron
9. Basket trap
10. Fish weir

How to make fishing net

Follow these steps to make an effective fishing net.

1. Fold the length of the cord in half from the center.
2. Slide fold over the dowelling and pull it down a bit, so you see the loop below dowelling.
3. Take both ends of the cord and pass them through the loop.
4. Pull tight to make a lark knot
5. Keep trying these knots with the same cord to make a fishing net finally

How to make a fishing pole and line

Making a fishing pole is moderately easy. Follow these steps:

1. Break off a 6-7 feet tree branch from a tree.
2. Clear the shoots, leaves, and side branches from the tree branch.
3. Use your fishing line to string the pole
4. Tie the line at the midpoint of your pole and wrap around it a couple of times
5. The end of the line should be tied around the tip of your fishing pole
6. Lastly, carve a hook on your fishing pole for hanging bait

How to find bait

Finding bait is very important as it is used to lure fish. The easiest way is to flip over rocks and other solid objects. You can find worms, slugs, grubs, and other bugs. You can use a hooked tool to scoop some mud, as there are many creatures like bloodworms hiding there. Tear into the soft, punky wood to find hidden grubs and beetles. Moreover, you can also force underground worms to come out by making vibrations into the ground.

Trot/jug lines

A trotline is a fishing tool that has multiple small dropper lines attached to a mainline. The droppers have a hook. There are many variations of trotlines worldwide like basic trotline tethered; trotline with weights, trotlines with floats in between, and so on.

A fishing jugline is used for deep waters, drop-offs, vertical fishing structures, and different feeding depths for fish. Jugline can be set up in many ways; the easiest way to set it up is by securing it to the bank with a line.

How to clean and cook a fish

Cleaning the fish is very important as eating without cleaning can be deadly. Most people like to clean their fish thoroughly and take out all the internal organs.

Use a knife to gut your skin and make an incision from the anus to the fish's bottom jaw. Be careful that you do not puncture any organs as it will ruin your fish. Now, you can keep the head if you want, or you can remove it. It's up to your liking. Peel out all the internal organs carefully.

Now, you can get started with cooking fish. There are multiple ways to do it. But in a situation like yours, you will probably only be able to make use of the most primitive method of cooking. This method only requires a fire, a sharpened stick, and fish. For this method to work best, do not fillet your fish. You can cook over an open fire, but since the heat is uneven, it can overcook some parts of your fish while not cooking some parts of your fish properly—a better way to cook it over coals.

TRACKING ANIMALS

Tracking animals should not be very difficult. Being quiet and patient are the most important things in tracking animals.

Animal footprints

Now, simply look for animal footprints. If you find a trail of footprints, you can follow it to find the animal. But if you do not have a proper footprint trail, it is time to look for other signs. Look for trails and runs; animals regularly use these paths and have many signs of an animal presence nearby.

Animal dung

You can also look for animal dung lying around on the ground. It gives you an incredible amount of information, such as the animal's size and even its diet.

Other important signs to locate animals are deer rubs on the trees, clumps of hair and feathers, gnaw marks, and chew marks.

TRAPPING

What animals can I catch?

Most people automatically imagine that when surviving in the wilderness, they will be eating large animals all the time. But the truth is you will probably be eating insects and other small animals mostly. These animals are swift and can be annoying. Therefore, make sure you know how to make effective traps.

Deadfall traps

A variety of deadfall traps can be made, but they all follow the same principles. A heavy object like a rock or log is propped up using the construction of sticks. It is designed so that the construction will fall when an animal comes in contact with it.

Trapping pits

Trapping pits are simple holes dug into the ground to trap an animal when it falls inside. It should be deep enough to ensure that the animal does not escape.

How to make a snare and where to place it?

Make a loop noose from a wire. Place this snare right outside the animal den. When an animal gets out of the den, its head will get stuck in the noose.

What bait do I use to lure animals?

You must choose an attractive bait to lure animals successfully. Now, your bait will vary depending on the type of animal you're targeting. Some generally used baits are:

- Marshmallows for raccoons
- Cabbage for rabbits
- Peanuts for squirrels
- Cantaloupe for groundhogs
- Canned fish for skunks or opossums
- Cat food for feral cats

Butchering animals

Proper butchering and meat preparation are very important as an improperly butchered animal can lead to sickness or even death. Animals have a large number of bacteria living inside. While butchering, you must make sure that such gut bacteria do not contaminate other parts of the animal. Moreover, the animal should be butchered right after it is killed to avoid decay.

The first step is to clean the animal. Remove the internal organs from the body cavity. Then, using a sharp knife, skin the animal. Small animals can be cooked whole, but larger animals must be butchered. Make sure your cuts on the meat are tender with less sinew.

What parts do I eat?

You can eat most parts of the animal, but taking out internal organs might be a good idea as they can be unhealthy for you. For instance, you can eat all the meaty parts like leg, rump, loin, flank, neck, and shoulder when it comes to deer. Just stay away from the gut as it has lots of bacteria in it.

How do I package it?

You will need to smoke or jerk the meat immediately if you do not have the means to refrigerate it. If you need to travel a long way after butchering meat, use salt to preserve it as it naturally kills bacteria.

What do I do with the hide?

You can use hides for footwear, upholstery, and leather goods. They will keep you warm out there in the wilderness.

GARDENING

You cannot solely rely on eating animals; you also must eat lots of vegetables and fruits to nourish your body with essential nutrients.

What to grow

Since your goal is to survive, you must ensure that there is nothing useless in your garden; every plant should be useful. Grow mixed vegetables and fruits for good nutrition. You can grow multiple herbs for flavor and medicinal uses. For crops, you can grow some starchy and sugary foods to fulfill your calorie requirements. However, growing green vegetables, fruits, and legumes are equally important as they are protein and essential vitamins and minerals.

When to plant

Most of the vegetables and fruits are seasonal crops and cannot be grown in other seasons. Cool-season vegetables like cabbage, onions, and potatoes grow best when temperatures range between 40 to 75 degrees Fahrenheit. Warm-season vegetables like peppers, okra, and corn do not perform well at temperatures below 50 degrees Fahrenheit as they are damaged by frost.

How much to grow

You should grow crops that are just enough for you and your fellow survivors. Make sure that nothing is wasted. You can't exactly know how much to grow at the start, as it will take experience. Some available quantities for four-person families are 40 asparagus plants, five broccoli plants, five brussels sprouts plants, five cabbage plants, and so on.

How to make compost

Items like kitchen scraps and straw or grass clippings give off carbon and nitrogen and make composts. To make compost, you must have 1-part green item for every 4-part brown item to make the best compost.

Make your compost in a dump bin, barrel, or pile. Add the browns and greens in. Keep turning over the pile once a week using a shovel. After it gets hot enough, it will turn dark. It is ready to be used now.

Saving seeds for future use

You cannot let any seeds go to waste as they are crucial for your survival. Most open-pollinated varieties are easy to store, hybrid varieties can go bad easily.

Save your seeds in tightly sealed glass containers for future use. The seeds stay dry and cool. You can further add silica-gel or milk as a desiccant to absorb moisture from the air, ensuring that seeds remain dry.

Orchard management

Sustaining your garden will not be an easy task. You must design your garden in a way that:

- It harbors an ideal habitat for chickens
- Has enough portion of chicken's diet
- Eliminates odors
- It does not require extreme human labor input
- Provides a good output of organic fresh fruit and vegetables
- It does not waste any space
- Has trees for defense and protection

BUILDING A ROOT CELLAR

A root cellar is a cool, dark storage space used to keep food cool and avoid food spoiling. The entrance of the root cellar should be big enough for you to walk in. It shouldn't be long-distance from your house. It should be large enough to store everything you need to store. Your root cellar should also have an adequate drainage system. You can also add shelves and storage containers.

You can modify garbage cans, old refrigerators, garages, basement, and cob and earth bags to use as root cellars.

Foraging for food (Knowing what's safe to eat)

You can't just eat anything to survive. You will need healthy crops and safe animals. Some crops and animals can even end up poisoning you. Therefore, you must gather safe and edible plants and animals. Foraged food is easy to obtain, and it contains higher levels of nutrients than commercial foods.

What wild plants, berries, fruits, roots, nuts, and mushrooms can I safely eat?

Here is a list of foods you can safely eat:

- Apples
- Peaches
- Grapes
- Pears
- Chokecherries
- Currants
- Crabapples
- Citrus fruit
- Berries of all types, such as strawberries, raspberries, blueberries, and blackberries.
- Wild greens
- Tubers
- Rice

What insects are safe to eat (and which ones should you avoid) and how to prepare them

Safe insects: grasshoppers and crickets, ants, larvae, earthworms, roly-poly, locust, cockroach, dragonfly, June bug, cicadas, termites

Insects to avoid: slugs and snails, tarantulas and scorpions, bees and wasps, caterpillars.

How to prepare insects: First of all, wash the insects. You can choose to boil, steam, or fry them. Cook them in whatever way for at least five minutes. Eat the insects immediately after preparing or preserve them in a refrigerator if you want to eat later.

COOKING FROM SCRATCH

How to make butter

You just need a canning jar and heavy cream to make butter from scratch. Fill half the jar with cream. Put a lid over it and start shaking. After some minutes of shaking, you will find a yellow clump of butter and some thin liquid. Rinse the butter with cold water.

How to use lard

Lard is one of the most useful survival foods.

- You can use it for deep frying, thanks to its high melting and smoking point. Some important uses are:
- You can apply it to your body as a suntan lotion to block harmful sun rays
- You can make candles from lard
- It can be used as a lip balm
- You can make deodorant from lard

Cooking without electricity

To be able to cook without electricity is
going to be one of the most crucial survival
techniques. In most end-of-the-world
situations, you won't find any electricity.
So, you should get right on learning to cook
without electricity. The most useful options
are:

- Use a grill with coals under it
- Find yourself a camping stove
  with at least two-burner stoves
- Fireplace
- Campfire
- You can hang a cast iron pot over a fire

Cook over an open fire

Simply cooking over an open fire is one of the most basic and oldest techniques.
However, cooking over an open fire can be tricky as it gives uneven heat to the food.
Therefore, keep turning over your food to regulate heat evenly. Get the right firewood
that will burn properly. Also, avoid cooking the food for longer times as it can drain
your food of essential nutrients.

Preserving food

There will be times when you find yourself
with excess food that you can't allow to
waste. Therefore, you must be aware of the
following preservation techniques.

- Canning Your Food
- Dehydrating Food
- Salt food
- Smoke food
- Pickling food
- Making jam and jellies

Survival food of our ancestors

Sadly, people have forgotten the old ways. Our ancestors have left us with food recipes that are very healthy and flavorful. The foods they consume are far more nutritious than the regular food you'll find today in markets.

Two of the best survival foods of our ancestors are:

Hardtack: It is brick-like resilient food that is loaded with a good deal of nutrition. It is made from very simple ingredients. You'll need 600 g of wheat flour, 2 cups of water, and three teaspoons of salt.

Pemmican: It is probably the strangest meatball you can ever eat. It is made from a mixture of two or three main ingredients. Dried jerky pounded into dust, rendered animal fat, and fruits/berries are the main ingredients.

WATER

FINDING DRINKABLE WATER

Knowing where to find healthy water is not only a good thing when you're out in the wild on a hot day, but it could also be a surviving technique in a situation where you have no other choice. If you find yourself in such a situation, first of all, try to remain as calm as possible. Do NOT panic. Take time to assess your situation calmly.

You will find three types of water resources: surface water like lakes and rivers, groundwater of springs, and rainwater. The most important quality you need in that body water is signs of life. Look for green vegetation nearby or animal tracks. If other living beings can drink from it, you probably can, too. Therefore, clear water does not mean drinkable water. Running water sources are the healthiest choices.

How to know if it is safe

There shouldn't be any pollution in the water source. Look around the water body for any contaminants or animal carcasses. They can infect water with harmful bacteria. Do not drink from water bodies around urban areas as they are likely to have contaminants from factories or industrial complexes.

PURIFYING WATER

Having pure water to drink is one of the top priorities in an emergency. The human body cannot last more than three days without any drinking water. Luckily, there are abundant water sources worldwide, and you can learn multiple ways to disinfect water from those sources. In case you can't find pure drinking water, you should purify impure water.

Ways of purifying water

1. Boiling: The most basic step to purify water is to boil it. It kills off dangerous parasites, bacteria, and other pathogens. Five minutes of boiling are enough to kill most bacteria but boil for ten minutes to be on the safe side.
2. Distillation: The safest solution to purify dangerous water is to distill it. It will remove any radiation, lead, salt, heavy metals, and other contaminants from the water. Water is turned into steam during distillation which can be captured in a separate container to create relatively clean water.
3. Filters: You can use pump-action filters or drip/suction filters to obtain clean drinking water. A pump-action filter forces water through a filter cartridge, whereas a drip/suction filter uses a gravity drip action to filter water.
4. UV light devices: UV light can be used as a disinfection method as it is very damaging to small organisms.
5. SODIS: Solar water disinfection (SODIS) is a water purification technique that employs energy from the sun to disinfect water. The most basic technique is to expose water in plastic bottles in the sun for at least one day. Almost all the biological hazards in water are killed off by UV light from the sun.
6. Disinfecting tablets: These are 99 percent effective in killing water-borne pathogens. However, it leaves a bad taste in the water. Also, it is not very good for pregnant women.
7. Chemicals: Household chemicals like bleach or iodine can be used to obtain clean water. Iodine can be harmful to some people; therefore, bleach is the better choice. Coldwater needs higher quantities of chemicals. After putting in the chemical, place a lid on the water container and shake it for some minutes. Place the bottle in a dark place for at least 3o minutes.

Active charcoal for water purification

Activated charcoal is a special type of charcoal used as a filter to purify water. When water is poured on activated charcoal, adsorption binds impurities on the charcoal's surface. It does not strip water of any important salts and minerals. Moreover, it will make your water taste better as it eliminates chlorine and other odors from the water. Active charcoal is quite cheap and also easy to maintain. You can use the same filter for 12 months.

BUILDING A WELL

Building a well will allow you to stock up on water during disaster scenarios. A well consists of a good hole, well casing, steining, well curb, well cap, well screen, pump, and a vessel for water retrieval.

How to know where to dig

Selecting a good site for building well is very important. You can't just build a well at any spot as it can deliver either unclean water or insufficient amounts of water. The key factors to consider for site selection are:

- Location: It should be near your house as carrying water from the well can be very troublesome.
- Access to utility and raw materials: Your well should not be very far from the place where you will get your raw materials from. It will be highly profitable and time-saving for you.
- Security: It should be in a place where it's safe from surrounding animals and insects to avoid contamination.
- Soil type: Soil must not be very hard as it will be difficult for you to dig on your own

How to build a well

Building a well will allow you to get drinking water and be used for irrigation purposes. There are many ways to build a well.

- Hand-dig: This is the simplest yet toughest and most time-consuming method. Shovels, buckets, picks, hatchets, and adzes are the commonly used tools for this method. It does not require any special talent; you should just swing a tool with basic coordination. An important thing to remember is that the well should be wide enough to accommodate the worker(s) inside. This type of well is mostly 50 feet deep.

- Sand pointing: In this method, a sharpened metal point at the end of a perforated pipe is thrust into the ground using a sledgehammer. It can be completed in a few hours. This type of method is only useful for sandy areas or areas where the soil is very soft.
- Sludging: This is an ancient method of digging a well in which a gantry is erected by which an open-topped pipe is rigged up to be lowered and raised consistently with a lever. This method is also only useful for areas with soft soil.
- Manual auger: This method employs a device that looks like a bucket with the bottom cutaway with a lower rim lined with sharp, cutting teeth. This drill is pushed into the soil and consistently spun around to dig a hole.

HYGIENE

Personal hygiene is taking care of your body and your surroundings. In a survival situation, maintaining personal hygiene will be even more important than in normal conditions. Your body can become vulnerable to multiple medical conditions in the wild. Maintaining good hygiene will reduce the spread of illnesses and the risk of medical complications.

Personal hygiene includes:

- Cleaning body every day
- Washing hands with soap or sanitizing after using the toilet
- Washing hands with soap or sanitizer after touching animals
- Brushing teeth two times a day
- Covering mouth and nose with a tissue or hand when coughing or sneezing.
- Regularly washing genitals
- Preventing body odor
- Preventing bad breath
- Handling food safely

You must take care of everything mentioned above to remain healthy. It will prevent you and the people around you from catching or spreading germs and harmful infectious diseases. Germs can be transmitted by touching other people, handling contaminated food, getting feces on the hands, or touching any dirty surface.

Bad personal hygiene can lead to the following conditions:

- Diarrhea
- Respiratory infections such as cold and flu
- Staph infection
- Worm-related condition
- Scabies
- Covid and other viral diseases

- Trachoma
- Athlete's foot
- Tooth decay

HUMAN WASTE

Defecating is a natural human process. Safely getting rid of human waste is important as human waste is very important.

How to make an outhouse/privy

An outhouse or a privy is a separate building from the main house used for privacy to cover a dry toilet or pit latrine. An outhouse is referred to by many names: a latrine, john, privy, or loo, and porta potty. You might find yourself in situations where water is limited or even unavailable. An outhouse is ideal for such conditions as it works without a sewer connection and flushing water. Outhouses are very common in third-world countries where proper sewage systems are not established.

The great thing about such dry toilets is that you can also compost your dry waste and use it as a fertilizer. A toilet specifically designed to make compost within the pit is called an Arborloo.

Types of outhouses

- Surface privy: It is a square box with a hole cut into the top, and it has no bottom. You can add a seat with a lid to the hole if available. After each use, some cover material such as wood ash is dumped through the hole onto the washer. The waste falls on the surface of the ground through the hole.
- Pit style outhouse: Dig a 2 feet square hole and make sure all the sides of the hole are even. Place a concrete or wooden box into the hole. You can wrap the box in tar paper to keep all the moisture out. Make a foundation of treated wood around the perimeter of the hole.

Location

The first thing to consider when planning to build an outhouse is the location. It should be at a location that will not pollute any water supply. You can build your outhouse on the downslope of the water supply and at least at a distance of 100 feet from the supply. Also, you want to build your outhouse away from your residence and preferably in a shaded area. Another important thing to keep in mind is that cleaning out waste should be easy. Try to build your outhouse on a gentle slope.

How to use cloth diapers

Cloth diapers are usually made from cotton; they are extremely absorbent. They can be washed and bleached since they are made for a pretty heavy-duty purpose. You can also reinforce your cloth diapers with several layers down the middle third when absorbance is the priority.

Some uses of cloth diapers are:

- Bandages: Cloth diapers are very resilient as they are flat and can be folded and molded to fit wherever you need them. You can fasten down cloth diapers on your wounds.
- Ice packs: Pull the polyacrylate out of your diaper by putting it in a Ziploc bag. Add a cup of alcohol and water. It is now ready to be used as an ice pack.
- Water filtration: Cloth diapers are perfect for filtering water as they are made with tightly woven fibers to help stop leaks.
- Cooling towels: In a survival situation, you might find yourself extra vulnerable to the dangers of heatstroke. Diapers are designed to hold moisture in; therefore, they can be used as a cooling towel.

MAKING SOAP

As we have firmly established, maintaining personal hygiene is very important. In crises, you will not be able to buy soaps from the market. Therefore, it is a good idea to know how to make your soap at home. It will take you a little experimentation and trial and error. Undoubtedly, making soap takes quite a bit of effort, but it can certainly be done without modern technology.

So, you will need these5 ingredients to make basic soap.

- Salt
- Wood ash
- Animal fats
- Plant oils
- Water

Step 1

To get started, get an acidic solution, also known as lye water. Lye water can be made by combining water and wood ashes. Burn wood to recover the ashes to make lye. Make sure you have a fire, so you get super white ashes. Gather the finest of ash after the fire is out and cold. Do not pick up any wood chips. Place it in a wood or plastic container.

Step 2

Water obtained from a spring, from rain, or even distillation is called soft water. It does not have any metallic or acidic chemicals in it.

Step 3

Boil some water and pour it inside the bucket of ashes. Now add some more soft water. Let this mixture cool down overnight. Separate the ash from lye water, use the technique of straining or sifting.

Step 4

Test your lye water's strength is proper. An egg or potato should float just below halfway.

Step 5

Get some animal fat. Make sure the fat is used right after hunting an animal, as animal fat goes rancid pretty quickly. Melt the fat to separate the greases. Pour the melted grease into the container by straining cloths. Add an equal amount of water and boil. Let the mixture cool down.

Step 6

Remove the dirty stuff after the fat hardens, leaving only the clean. This hardened fat can be stored for a couple of weeks for future use. Now, you need to add correct proportions of grease to lye which is 1:12 respectively.

Step 7

Let this new soap rest in the bucket for two days. There you go, your soap is ready! Cut into small bars and let it dry out.

Handwashing clothes

Since now you know how to make a bar of soap, it is time to learn how to put that soap to good use. There is a good chance you will not have any modern washing machine; you're going to have to do your laundry manually. Follow these simple steps:

1. Fill a big container with water
2. Submerge and soak your clothes in it
3. Rinse and repeat

Toilet paper Alternatives

Everyone is a big fan of toilet paper in their houses. But you will eventually run out of your toilet paper supply in a crisis. You must have a clear picture of your possible options for replacing toilet paper.

1. Flannel squares
2. Bidet
3. Washcloths
4. Worn out socks
5. Spray bottle
6. Baby wipes
7. Wooly lamb's ear
8. Mullein leaves
9. Tree leaves
10. Newspapers
11. Corncobs
12. Pine needles and cones
13. Snow
14. Cardboard toilet paper rolls
15. Hand

MEDICINE

So far in this book, we have talked about how to take the best care of yourself, but it is time now to assume the worst. Since crises are so unpredictable, even after taking all the right steps, there's a chance you will get sick someday. So, you should know how to take care of yourself then!

HERBAL REMEDIES

In a survival situation, when you run out of medicine, herbal remedies will make all the difference between a full recovery or a sad death to an infection, illness, injury, or disease. Here, take a look at some of the clinically proven herbal remedies that could one day save your life.

1. Garlic: It is super powerful in alleviating and treating several health issues like flu, dental pain, skin disorders, pain from arthritis, tumors, blood glucose concentration.
2. Marigold: It can help rejuvenate your skin by acting against rashes, inflammations, eczema, and even ulcers.
3. Cordyceps: It improves energy level, heart health, oxygen uptake, and the respiratory system overall.
4. Aloe vera: It is known for its advanced healing properties for treating burns. It can be applied as a gel.
5. Ginseng: According to PubMed, it can alleviate insomnia, palpitations, anorexia, and shortness of breath.
6. Rosemary: It can help you with stomach cramps, boost your immune system and memory and focus, fight cancer and reduce hair loss.
7. Ginger: It is enriched with gingerol, which helps prevent cancerous cells from spreading, treats nausea and seasickness, lowers blood sugar, fixes indigestion, and boosts the immune system.
8. Echinacea: It can help you with common cold, random headaches, stomach cramps, and toothaches.

9. Yarrow: It is easy to grow and helps with cold, fever, cramps, stomach aches, and slow healing wounds.
10. Basil: It is rich in essential oils which help digestion, counteract bloating, and reduce blood pressure.

MAKING YOUR ANTIBIOTICS

Penicillin was the very first antibiotic and helped in maintaining good health. It can be very hard to make penicillin safely without having the correct knowledge.

Step 1. Isolate Penicillin bacteria

Place a piece of bread in a dark place in a closed container at 70 degrees Fahrenheit. Wait for a bluish-green mold to appear.

Step 2. Re-culture penicillin

Boil slices of unpeeled potato in distilled water for 30 minutes. Use a cheesecloth to strain the contents. Add 20g of sugar and agar each. Then add water until the total volume is 1 liter. Pour this mixture into Petri dishes and cover them immediately.

Step 3. Streak your petri dish

Bend a thin piece of wire into an oval shape. Touch the tip of the wire to the mold. Heat it to the point it gets red hot. Drip it into a broth mixture to cool it down. Form 3 lines on a petri dish.

Step 4. Let penicillin grow

Allow penicillin to grow in covered Petri dishes.

Step 5. Ferment your penicillin

Ferment penicillin spores for maximum reproduction

Step 6. Extract penicillin

After a week, your penicillin should now be fermented. Strain the liquid part with a coffee filter or sterilized cheesecloth. Let the liquid rest in a sterile container. Test the pH of penicillin, and it should be around 5. Keep adding drops of hydrochloric acid until the pH drops to 2.2.

Step 7. Further extract

Dissolve ethyl acetate in pure penicillin. Place the solution in a ventilated area; the ethyl should evaporate. You are now left with a pure extract of penicillin.

NATURAL PAINKILLERS

1. Wild lettuce

It is widely known as opium lettuce as it is such a potent painkiller. It can be used as:

- Tea – 1 tsp. Of dried lettuce seeped in a cup of water
- Resin - 1.5 grams of resin as needed.
- Smoking – 0.25 grams
- Tinctures – 12-24 drops per day
2. Turmeric

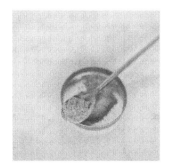

It contains curcuminoid compounds with numerous health benefits like reducing inflammation, boosting cardiovascular health, and helping with depression. As a painkiller, it treats GI disorders and inflammatory conditions. It can be used as:

- Tea – mix with oil and black pepper
- Topical – make an ointment by mixing it with oil
- Dried powder – mix with oil and black pepper to increase absorption
3. White willow bark

It is considered nature's aspirin as it is enriched with salicylic. It treats inflammatory and muscular pains. It can be used as:

- Chewing – chew off the bark directly

- Tea – pain-killing benefits if drank lots every day
- Tincture – 1-2 drops per day
4. Lavender

It has great calming effects and works as a potent natural painkiller too. It reduces joint pain, toothache, migraine pain, muscle pain, and more. It can be used as:

- Inhalation – 2-4 drops of lavender oil in 3 cups of boiling water
- Topical – toxic when taken orally.
- Tincture – 2-4 ml three times every day
5. Clove

It has amazing abilities to treat toothaches, joint and muscle pains. It can be used as:

- Tincture – Mix with a carrier oil and apply
- Smoking – Helps with pain but is very toxic
- Dried powder – Mix with water and drink
6. Kava kava

It helps relieve anxiety and pain from sore muscles. It takes a long time to grow but has very rewarding health benefits. It can be used as:

- Capsule – put dried flowers into capsules
- Smoking – dosage amount varies
- Tincture – take 40ml daily
- Tea – use 5 grams for 1 cup
7. Marijuana

It has benefits like reducing anxiety and upset stomach. Larger can get you high, though. It can be used as:

- Oil
- Tincture
- Smoking
- Vaporizing

SIMPLE FIRST AID

Life in crises can be so unpredictable that you should always be prepared for the worst-case scenarios. Learning basic first aid skills should be one of your top priorities.

1. CPR: Cardiopulmonary resuscitation is one of the most important and useful first aid skills. The standard procedure of CPR has been changed drastically. Now you have to skip the breathing portion and focus on chest compressions. It is hands-only CPR now.

2. Making a splint: A couple of sticks and duct tape or a pillowcase or towel can accomplish immobilizing a broken or sprained bone. The person will be able to move with decreased pain, and recovery will happen faster.

3. Cleaning and dressing wound: Know how to lacerate and properly wrap the wound. Sometimes you will be required to do a butterfly stitch to close the wound properly.

4. Heimlich maneuver: If you are being choked, wrap your arms around the person while standing behind and make several swift jabs upward as it will help dislodge something that has blocked their airway.

5. Treating shock: People do not realize this, but people die from shock sustained from any traumatic event or injury. Learn how to recognize shock symptoms. Knowing how to keep a person calm, their feet elevated, and their body warm can help maintain their blood pressure.

6. Stopping the bleeding: Being able to recognize the arterial bleeds and stop the bleeding is very critical. You should be able to use pressure to stop bleeding in combination with bandages. As a last resort, a tourniquet can be used too.

7. Treating hypothermia: Hypothermia is very common in survival conditions. You should be able to recognize the signs of hypothermia and know how to treat it quickly.

8. Treating heat strokes: If you find someone suffering from heat exhaustion, you should push fluids, place a cool cloth on the back of the neck and keep the person in the shade as it helps drop the body temperature immediately.

9. Treating burns: A person can lose several layers of skin, depending on the severity of the burn. You should know how to treat 2nd, and 3rd degree burns with cream and how to bandage.

HOW TO MAKE YOUR TOOTHPASTE

Making toothpaste is not very hard. You will only need baking soda, sea salt, bentonite clay, coconut oil, natural sweeteners, and some essential oils. Follow these recipes.

Recipe 1

- 1/4 cup of baking soda
- 1/8 cup of sea salt
- 10 drops of peppermint or cinnamon oil
- 1/4 cup of filtered water

Recipe 2

- 1/4 cup of coconut oil
- 1/4 cup of baking soda
- 10-20 of drops essential oils
- 5 drops of stevia

Recipe 3

- 1/4 cup of bentonite clay
- 2 tbsp. Of calcium powder
- 3 tbsp. Of coconut oil
- 1/2 tsp of sea salt
- 1 tsp of baking soda
- 10-20 drops of essential oil
- 5 drops of sweetener
- 1/2 cup of filtered water

Recipe 4

- 3 tbsp. Of bentonite clay
- 1/2 tsp of sea salt

- 1 tsp of baking soda
- 2 tbsp. Of coconut oil
- 20 drops of essential oil
- 5 drops of sweetener, or to taste
- 3 tbsp. Of filtered water

Recipe 5

- 1/4 cup of coconut oil
- 1/4 cup of bentonite clay
- 3 tbsp. Of filtered water
- 1 tsp of sea salt
- 10-20 drops peppermint oil
- 4 or 5 of drops stevia or xylitol (optional)

MIDWIFERY – HOW TO DELIVER A BABY

We all are so dependent on hospitals to deliver our babies today. We can't even think about delivering babies on our own. But it is not that difficult; it is very natural. You can learn to do it by following these simple tips.

- Stay active: As contractions get closer together and more regularly, it becomes important for the woman to stay as upright and active as possible.
- Eat and drink lots: Think of labor as a marathon for which you need proper hydration and fuel to get through.
- Be patient: Let the natural labor process run its course. Do not rush.
- Get into position: As you get almost ready to deliver the baby, get into a good position for delivery like leaning or semi-squatting. Do not lie on your back!
- Don't pull: Let the baby come out at its own time and pace. Do not pull, as you can end up dislocating the baby's shoulder or causing even more lasting and irreversible damage.

- Cut the cord at the right time: Do not cut the umbilical cord right after the baby emerges as the placenta and cord continue to circulate blood for some time. Wait until the cord stops pulsing.

TRANSPORTATION

No question maintaining good transportation will form a key part of your plans when it comes to preparing for survival.

HOW TO REPAIR A VEHICLE

It is very important to know how to build, rebuild and scavenge parts. You must always keep an emergency repair kit with yourself in the trunk of your car. The repair tools include a good quality jack, wrenches, tire iron, rubber mallet, sled hammer, jumper cables, socket set, torque wrench, spare fuses, wire, cable, lubricant, and extra rags. You might encounter vehicle breakdowns during a crisis.

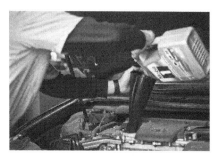

Here are the ten most important basic diagnostic and repair skills that you should know:

1. Change oil filter, oil, and air filter
2. Change tires
3. Change bleed brake lines and brake pads
4. Check the battery, its spark plugs, and distributor connections
5. Gap and change spark plugs and evaluate the timing
6. Change torque engine head bolts
7. Replace head gasket of engine
8. Repair minor leaks of radiator
9. Change alternator and starter
10. Test and replace belt systems
11. Wire dragging mufflers and pipes of exhaust systems
12. Change fuses

HOW TO CAPTURE AND TAME WILD HORSES

The ability to ride a horse in a post-apocalypse scenario can potentially be one of the most important survival tools. Power sources for movement and transportation will likely be limited or nonexistent; therefore, horsemanship skills will be essential.

Finding horses

Finding horses out in the wild is not the toughest job. Like most people, your biggest problem will be that you have never ridden or handled a horse before. Maybe you have watched some Western movies and seen bucking broncos and cowboys. And now it is time for you to get into action. Your survival might depend on this. Here is how to succeed.

Get some rope halters, soft rope to lead before you go out to find horses. If you happen to stumble on a herd of horses, do not just rush in. It is important to observe them from a distance and figure out who the herd leader is. Then walk in front of them, let them spot you. Do not move stealthily like a hunter; move normally, so they accept your presence.

Slowly approach the horses, let the leader smell your hand, and rub the horse's neck. Take few days before you put a lead around its neck. Allow yourself to become a common and friendly sight for the horse, keep bringing something to eat. The horse needs to trust you, or your whole effort will be in vain.

It is also possible that the horses you encounter are wild, American Mustangs. These are not domesticated; they avoid humans and can be a big challenge. It is important to have the right knowledge and attitude to make them partners in mutual survival. Wild horses should be approached with extra patience as they are wary of humans.

When they finally begin to embrace you, follow the same touch process and offer food. Do not make any sudden movements as it will result in the herd running away. You will have to work harder to win their trust.

Riding horses

All you need to ride a horse is your rope halter. You can start on a hackamore, a harness that exerts pressure on the nose area. It is one of the most sensitive areas of the horse. Use your legs and body to guide the horse; the reins only help in steering.

Try to use simple equipment for riding a horse as it will save you a lot of time and material. You do not need a saddle to ride. Bareback helps you stay in touch with the horse and keep you connected. It teaches balance and sensitivity, and your horse can read your body quite well.

How to make a horse wagon

Making a horse wagon is not particularly that difficult; it depends on your resources and skills. Once you figure out what kind of wagon you exactly want, you can get started. Ponder over how much weight you need to carry and how big your 'engine is.' Obtain measurements, specifications, and dimensions for the wagon.

Use marine plywood to take a seat for your wagon, upholster it with vinyl and foam. Find yourself two rubber-tired wheels if you can. Now comes the critical part, mounting the axles of the frame. Suppose it's possible, weld the axles at each end of a pipe that can be clamped under the frame. Or you can simply tie with a rope. For the frame, use a 1x2 inch rectangular steel tube.

You're now done with the main part; you have a comfortable seat on a stiff frame on two wheels. You just have to hook it up with the horse. Attach staves to each side of the frame at points wide enough apart for the horse to fit in. Lastly, attach your horse's harness and collar to the staves using bolts if available. Or you can simply tie it with ropes. Now, your horse wagon should be ready. It won't be the prettiest, but you can make good use of it.

SAFETY AND DEFENSE

We simply cannot overemphasize the importance of safety and defense. There will be bad people out there trying to hurt you. Your threats will only increase in a survival situation. The threat can be from wild animals or from your fellow humans who will be struggling to survive just like you. You might think an end-of-the-world event will erase all the bad people, but you're wrong. You should focus on learning important safety and self-defense techniques.

GUNSMITHING

Gunsmithing is not that difficult job; you just need to have the knowledge and some skills. So, you're going to have to learn how to design, build, modify, renovate and repair firearms. Except for these basic skills, you don't need to learn creative skills as you only need this for personal safety and defense. You have to be very careful when gunsmithing because if you are not, you might harm yourself or someone else. Beware of the following common mistakes:

- Incorrectly assembled
- Missing parts
- Cracks and other damage
- Not properly aligned
- Obstructions
- Issues with the firing pin
- Wear and tear

How do I make my rifle?

You should learn to make a customizable AR-15 rifle. A range of custom buildups can be made. You are going to need the following parts:

- 5.56/.223 Caliber
- 16' stainless or Chromoly barrel
- Carbine-length gas system
- Forged upper receiver
- Standard lower parts kit
- Standard buffer assembly
- Standard auto M16 bolt carrier group

Once you have these parts, you can build a reliable, affordable survival rifle using the AR-15 platform.

You will need these tools:

- 80 lower jig
- Handheld drill
- Hand router
- Drill press
- Drill bits
- End mill bit
- Table vise

It barely takes 2 hours to machine the lower receiver if you have the right tools and equipment. Find an AR-15 jig that has pre-drilled and pr-cut templates. These templates sit on top and sides of your receiver, so you'll know where to drill and cut.

After drilling and cutting the receiver blank, you can now install your lower parts kit, upper receiver, buffer assembly, gas system, barrel, and everything else. Your rifle can now be tested for use.

How do I make my ammo?

If you run out of your bullet stock, you can make homemade ammo. You need specific materials and supplies. First and foremost, get yourself safety gear because you have to work with hot stoves and liquid metals. Make sure you have a pair of safety goggles, heavy-duty gloves, and close-toed shoes.

Traditionally, lead has been used for making bullets, but it is too soft for modern handguns and rifles. You can mix the lead with a bit of tin to make it harder and easier to work with. If you do not have power, melt the lead and alloy over a campfire in an iron pot. Use a spoon to stir.

Now, get on to the fluxing stage. Add wax shavings/bullet lube to the melted alloy. Stir thoroughly and wait for impurities and steel shavings to collect. Dump the skimmed impurities into the steel pan. Gently pour the melted alloy in stainless-steel condiment cups to make ingots until a little over halfway; allow the alloy to cool down and solidify. Using your heavy gloves, turn the cups inside out so the ingot will fall out.

Reheat the ingots one or two at a time. Use a small iron spoon to put the melted alloy into the bullet mold. After a few seconds, open the mold and shake the bullets out.

How do I properly clean a gun?

Good care and maintenance of your gun will ensure that it is ready to be used when you need it. Clean and function-check your firearm now and then. Your gun cleaning kit should have the following items:

- Bore snake
- Jags
- Patches sized for the bore of your gun
- Bore brushes
- Cleaning rods
- Utility brush/old toothbrush
- Bore cleaner
- Gun lubricant/oil
- Cotton swabs
- Rags

To get started, unload your firearm, make sure the chambers are empty. Then disassemble your weapon. Use a bore snake to clean your bore. Brush and swab the barrel with just one pass. After this, gently spray the parts with a cleaner. Scrub with utility brushes and then follow with another light spray with more cleanser.

Use your rags to wipe them down until they come back clean. Gently, apply oil all over the firearms to the point that the part glistens but does not soak. Your firearm is now ready to be reassembled. To perform a function check after.

How to repair guns?

Gun repairing skills are essential for dodging a loss of capability to use the gun safely. Your gun can encounter the following problems:

- The firing pin gets worn out
- Mainspring breaks up
- The trigger return spring breaks up
- Corrosion
- Drift sight issues

HOW TO BE STEALTH

This is one of the most important skills in survival situations. You're going to have to be stealthy when catching animals. The slightest noise can ruin your animal hunting session. It takes a bit of experience to master the art of stealth, but you can get there with the right knowledge.

Fox walk

Believe it or not, this modern life has us moving all wrong. We walk in ways that put all the shock on our knees and hips; we sit too much, we slouch, and whatnot. Fox walk is not only healthy for you but also allows you to move stealthily. It doesn't exactly look like a fox walking. Here is a step-by-step tutorial on how to fox walk:

Step 1: Your knees are excellent shock absorbers; walking with bent knees cushions impact and gives you a lower profile. So, bend your knees.

Step 2: Take very short steps, consciously place each foot. Place your feet down only when you know it is safe.

Step 3: When you walk, point your feet forward. You will have more control and balance with your foot placement.

Step 4: Walk as straight as you can. It will keep your center of gravity in the same plane so that you won't draw any attention.

Step 5: Place the outer edge of the foot down quietly, rolling from the outer blade to the inside. Place the heel of the foot only after the full ball of your foot has made contact with the ground.

Step 6: Do so when you know it is safe to transfer your weight to the foot. Then, slowly pick up the back foot and move it forward.

Wide-angle vision

The conditions after an end-of-the-world event will require you to operate with a great amount of tunnel vision through activities such as horse-riding, hunting, cooking, and so on. Focusing with your eyes will allow you to direct your energy.

Wide-angle vision is a method that elevates the human ability to access alpha states. Benefits of alpha states include heightened awareness, increased creativity and intuition, peak physical performance, greater learning efficiency, and enhanced healing potential. In this state, your brain slows down and allows you to process more of what you see.

You can access wide-angle vision by deliberately choosing to pay attention to everything in your field of view while not paying attention to anything particularly. It gets your peripheral vision activated. Practice standing meditation; slow yourself down, relax breathing, look forward and raise your arms, wiggle your fingers, and notice your eyes focusing on the fingers.

HOW TO USE ROPE (OR PARACORD)

You might not have observed this before but try to observe whenever watching any survival movie; you will see ropes being used in some capacity at one point.

Ropes are extremely important; you can get the following uses out of a survival rope:

- Fishing
- Boot laces
- Climbing/hiking
- Sewing thread
- Building shelter
- Trying down tarp
- Holding gear together
- Building traps
- Flossing
- Tying things on top of the car
- Making tourniquet
- Building raft
- Building ladder
- And many more!

There are many types of ropes available in the market. It is important to understand the build quality and purpose of each rope to choose the best rope for your survival kit. Here are a few widely used types of ropes:

- Laid rope: The twisted rope also looks like a spiral and is usually made of three strands. Even though it is not the strongest nor the best rope design, it still has many uses.

- Braided rope is made by weaving fiber strands, and it comes in hollow or double braided styles. It mostly has marine applications, but on land, it rots very quickly; they don't stretch and unbraid well.
- Climbing ropes: It features a kernmantle design. Its inner core is made of separate strands, which makes it very strong.
- Guyline cord: These are pretty handy when lengthening or replacing a tent/tarp guyline, but it is not very reliable for other uses.
- Bungee cord: Also known as shock cord, it is a very elastic cord whose outer sheath is made of propylene or woven cotton.
- Sisal: It is made of stiff fibers. It does not cost much and copes very well with salty water.
- Paracord: The parachute cord is the most popular choice. It is made of lightweight nylon using kernmantle technology. It offers high strength, resilience, and flexibility.

KNOT TYING

The knots that you are about to learn about form the basic principles of knot tying.

- Figure 8 knot: It provides a quick and convenient stopper knot that will help prevent a line from sliding out of sight. It can also be undone easily.
- Half hitch: It intertwines the ends of two cords and is used in tying other knots.
- Noose knot: It does the job of a snare that is to catch small animals.
- Overhand knot: It can be used to prevent the end of a rope from unraveling.
- Sheet bend: It is used to join two ropes of unequal or similar size.
- Slip knot: Slip knot is a frequently used knot. It is used as a temporary stopper knot.
- Square knot: Basically, it is a simple way of joining two ropes made of two half knots. This is the knot we use to tie shoelaces.

TRADE

The people who were lucky enough to survive will have to cooperate to survive. Trading is going to play an important role. We are not talking about ordinary trading for the money you see today. You see, the thing is, all your money is going to be useless if you find yourself in a survival situation. You're going to have to shift back to the ancient trading system, a system that has been in place as early as the inception of humanity. The system is known as barter.

HOW TO BARTER

Bartering is a very effective way to acquire goods and services that you cannot directly get by yourself. Bartering is trading, but no money is required to conduct transactions. So, what you do in bartering is trade a good or service in return for a good or service of similar value.

Start practicing your barter skills today; you do not have to wait for a crisis. It is very helpful even in a normal situation. And in crises, bartering will help you build good relationships with your fellow survivors. You can be useful to each other. What skill you have, someone might not have, and vice versa. So, you can trade to fill each other's needs.

SKILLS TO TRADE

Following is a list of useful skills that will be in demand during crises.

- **Plumbing**: You can specialize in installing and maintaining systems used for potable water and drainage and sewage in plumbing systems. You can go and fix the plumbing systems of your fellow survivors' homes in return for their services or goods.
- **Security**: In survival conditions, security is going to be a big concern. Security from wild animals, rogue survivors, and other threats is going to be very important. You will already be low on resources, and you cannot afford anyone stealing your stuff; you can't afford to get attacked by wild

animals. People are going to need security, and you can provide it to them. You can stand guard for them at night, and if you have a rifle, that is even better.

- **Soap Making and Candle Making**: Believe us, soap and candles will be in high demand if the disaster goes on long enough. People need to take care of their hygiene; they will need good quality soap for that. Moreover, since you'll likely have no electricity, candles will become very popular as people need light in the nighttime to perform their tasks.

- **Water Purification**: Access to pure water will be very hard, and not everyone can purify water on their own. If you know how to purify water, you can do it for your fellow survivors in return for their services or goods.

- **Welding**: Welding is an important skill that is made use of frequently. You can help repair parts of people's homes, vehicles with the use of welding.

- **Carpentry**: It is the art and trade of cutting, working, and joining timber. You're going to have to build new wooden objects as time goes on. Your old tables might wear out; you will need to have them fixed. You might need new objects.

- **Home Brewing Your Beer**: Everyone likes the good 'Ol beer. Of course, as time passes, people are going to run out of their alcohol stock. If you know the art of brewing beer, believe us, you're going to be very popular. People are going to want to trade with you for your beer.

- **Beekeeping**: You can even maintain bee colonies in self-made hives. Bees are kept to collect their honey and beeswax, flower pollen, bee pollen, and propolis. These products are going to be a luxury and will be in high demand.

- **Tanning leather**: Skins and hides of animals that can be used to produce leather have many uses. It is going to be tough to survive out in the cold without electricity and modern tools. Therefore, leather is going to come in handy in keeping you warm. You can tan the skins of animals you hunt and provide them to your fellow survivors.

- **Blacksmithing**: You can create multiple objects from wrought iron or steel by forging. You can make objects like gates, railings, grilles, furniture, sculpture, decorative and religious items, cooking utensils, and weapons.

These items are going to be in demand as they are frequently used in our day-to-day lives.

- **Gunsmithing**: It is not that difficult a job; you just need to have good knowledge and some skills. So, you're going to design, build, modify, renovate and repair firearms. Except for these basic skills, you don't need to learn creative skills as you only need this for safety and defense purposes.
- **Sewing, Knitting and Crocheting**: Being able to fix clothes is indeed a very useful skill. In survival conditions, you will not be able to buy commercially produced clothes; you're going to have to stick with the clothes you have. Now, these clothes are bound to be a victim of wear and tear as time passes by. You can fix these clothes by sewing, knitting, and crocheting.

- **Weaving and Spinning**: If your clothes are completely ruined, you will need to weave and spin new clothes. People are eventually going to need new clothes, but not everyone has the skill of weaving and spinning so that you can do it for them.
- **Cleaning**: Having a clean environment is a big part of maintaining good hygiene. You can help people clean their homes, gardens, and vehicles.
- **Construction**: A disastrous event may lead to destroying lots of property. You and other survivors might have to start from square one, meaning construct your homes and other useful buildings again. Or you simply might need to construct other home objects. Shelter is indeed the most important factor in your survival. If you do not have a good shelter, you will be vulnerable to nature's dangers.
- **Cooking**: Say goodbye to buying ready-made food from stores. People will have to cook their food. Not everyone will know about cooking survival food. You can use cooking as a barter skill.
- **Medical/Dental/First Aid**: People are bound to get medical issues in survival conditions no matter how much care people take. Taking care of people in case of injuries, diseases, and toothaches are going to be very important.

- **Gardening**: Gardening is a very important skill that everyone should. You should be able to grow your fruit, vegetables, herbs, and spices as you can't find everything out there. You can do this for others too.
- **Mechanic**: You can help people fix their vehicles. Vehicles will be prone to issues more frequently in crises.

OTHER SKILLS

POWER GENERATION

So far, we have talked a lot about you
not having electricity in a survival
situation. But wait a minute, what if you
were to make your own? It is not as
difficult as it sounds. It does take
knowledge and skill, but it is certainly
possible. Here are two ways you can
generate electricity.

- Solar

Solar energy is the fastest-growing
energy alternative in many parts of the world. A beginner like you can apply the basic
principles to create a small solar cell.

Step 1. Obtaining titanium dioxide

Collect donut powder containing impure titanium dioxide. Stir the powder into warm
water and filter it to obtain titanium dioxide-free of sugars. To remove fat, heat the
powder at 500 degrees Fahrenheit for three hours.

Step 2. Creating solar cell

Coat a conductive glass with a solution of titanium dioxide and ethanol. Use a
dropper or pipette to land a very small amount of the solution. A microscope slide can
scrape off excess solution. Place the solar cell in a clear, heatproof container. Cook it
for 10 to 20 minutes on a hotplate. Finally, strain your solar cell with tea as the
compounds present in tea help in capturing sunlight.

Step 3. Generating electricity

Take another piece of conductive glass and color it with graphite. This works as a counter electrode. Place a spacer between this glass and the solar cell. Add an electrolyte solution such as iodine solution and alcohol in a 3:1 ratio. Gently press the two glasses together. Place it in sunlight to generate your very own electricity.

- Wind

If you are stranded in a windy area, you can certainly install a small wind electric system. You need to be able to:

1. Pour a proper cement foundation
2. Have access to a lift or way of erecting the tower
3. Know the difference between direct current and alternate current wiring
4. Safely wire the wind turbine
5. Know how to install batteries safely

If you possess the skills mentioned above, you are ready to install your electric wind system. Now you need to locate the best site for installing your system. You will have good access to the prevailing wind if you install your turbine on top or the windy side of the hill. You also need to consider existing obstacles like houses, trees, and sheds. Moreover, leave enough room to raise and lower the turbine for its maintenance.

NAVIGATING WITHOUT GPS

Knowing how to move from one place to another is going to be key in your survival. You might get lost; you will need to navigate your way back to your home. GPS is an amazing tool, but it might not work, or you simply might not have one. So, it is essential to know how to navigate without a GPS.

How to use a compass?

It is one of the most basic navigation tools. It requires no batteries, can work with any map or even without a map. You must be aware of the basic concepts of a compass to use it.

So, the first thing worth knowing is that the floating needle in the compass is magnetized. The red end will always point towards the magnetic north. No matter which direction you are facing, the needle points in the north.

However, it is important to note that the magnetic north is not true north (the North Pole). So, now you have two different months. The answer to this problem is declination. The difference in degrees between true north and magnetic north is known as declination. The amount of declination depends on your geographical location.

If you have a topographic map, it will most likely have a legend that shows declination as two straight lines. The line representing true north has a star on top of it, and the line representing magnetic north is indicated as MN. It is a good idea to type in your postal codes on the internet and find the exact declination for your area. The declination will be expressed in degrees west or degrees east. You can adjust your compass accordingly.

These are the main things to keep in mind when using a compass.

How to use a paper map?

It is always nice to have a paper map as a backup in emergencies or inconvenient situations. It might even become a norm for you to use the paper map in survival situations. Paper maps are quite easy to use. Just familiarize yourself with the key elements of a paper map to read it.

- Compass rose: Almost all maps have a compass rose, a visual feature to point you in the right direction. North is always at the top of the map.
- Index: An alphabetical list of locations is included on the side of most maps. There are number-letter combinations next to each entry that corresponds to a point on the map.

- Grid: A grid is the columns of letters along one side of the page and rows of numbers across the bottom or top. It makes it easier to pinpoint locations.
- Legend: It is a table on the side of a map that lets you know what each symbol, line, and color on the map represents.
- Scale: It is a line that is marked in inches and labeled with distances. It shows the ratio of the actual distance to the distance on the map.

COMMUNITY FELLOWSHIP

If you find yourself in a survival situation with a couple of other people, the key to your survival will be how well you get along with others. A good community has a network of individuals who possess the essential skills, talents, and resources to thrive during a crisis. Humans are designed to live in groups and depend on each other. You cannot survive on your own. You need to establish goodwill among  your community. There will be times when you need to put others first. For instance, someone will need more food than you at a given time, so you should give it to them.

Building a successful community will take planning and effort. Communicate with people as much as you can! Create networks with like-minded people, evaluate people who have good skills, stay away from negative people who have no use for you and will only create more troubles.

ENTERTAINING YOURSELF

One of the most challenging things in survival situations will be to spend spare time. Let's say, a few days have passed since the traumatic event, and now you've become self-sufficient. The next step is to learn to get comfortable and have fun in your new reality. Here are some fun-filled activities that can help you kill time:

- Play card gamer
- Read books
- Play survival board games
- Make puzzles
- Play instruments
- Play with the beach ball
- Badminton
- Fly kites
- Sing songs
- Organize skits
- Play camping games
  (scavenger hunt, hide and seek, truth or dare, and so on)
- Throw darts, knives, and shurikens
- Crossbows and bows
- Play with pets and farm animals
- Swings
- Skip ropes
- Make and play with origami boomerangs
- Drawing
- Phone or tablet (if you're lucky enough to have power)
- Birdwatching

PREDICTING THE WEATHER

Having to survive in the wild without any electricity and modern tools call for going out for long journeys to get what you need to survive. If you go out on days with bad weather, you will be doomed. Therefore, it is good to know how to predict the weather. Follow these tips to master the art of predicting the weather.

- Observe the clouds, the kids, and the shapes present in the sky. Whiter clouds indicate good weather.
- Keep check of air pressure by observing the smoke pattern coming from a campfire. If it goes straight up, that means there is high water pressure.
- Reading wind is key to forecasting weather. A gentle wind indicates clear weather.
- Observe if there is a visible ring around the sun or moon. If you see one, this signals the coming of bad weather.
- Observe the number of stars in the sky. Lesser stars mean more sky is covered with clouds.
- The behavioral pattern of birds also gives information about the weather. Birds only schedule migrations when the weather is good.

- Use a balsam fir tree to make a weather stick. It works similarly to a campfire's smoke.

STAYING CALM – AVOIDING THE URGE TO PANIC

Every skill that we have mentioned in this book takes much more than just knowledge and skill. To survive, you need to have a positive mental attitude. Without being mentally calm, no matter how much skill or knowledge you have, you simply cannot perform any task. In tough situations like these, you will have to control your urge to panic if you want to survive.

Follow these tips to avoid panicking:

- Know the signs of panicking
- Don't stop living your life
- Calmly talk to yourself, console yourself
- Acknowledge the issue, don't distract yourself
- Don't forget to breathe
- Keep your mind in the present reality
- Talk to others
- Exercise and sleep well

REPURPOSING ITEMS

In survival situations, you will come across many items that will seem useless, but you have to think creatively. You can reuse or recycle those items in ways you normally wouldn't.

Here are some items and their uses.

- Flour sacks: Flour sacks can be used in clothing. It could be sewn into just about anything. Patches can be made out of the flour sack and applied to pants and shirts.
- Rabbits are very versatile animals; you could feed them produce scraps or alfalfa, and they will still reproduce quickly. They could be

used for meat or sold to others for barter.

- Washtubs: Washtubs can be used for so many things such as washing dishes, washing clothes, or even water heaters.

- Presents: Presents can be made from any leftover material if you put your mind to it. Broken shoelaces could become woven key or watch fobs.

- Towels, sheets, and blankets: These valuable items can be cut up into dresses, curtains, or more patches for other sheets or pillowcases.

- Chickens: Like rabbits, chickens are also very versatile. Feathers from chicken can be used to make or repair blankets, pillows, or even saggy mattresses.

- Tires and inner tubes: If you are super desperate for heat, you can burn tires for heat. You can also cut tires to replace shoe bottoms or make swings for kids.

CONCLUSION

If you have reached this far, pat yourself on the back, you have now educated yourself about the forgotten survival skills of your ancestors. You probably understand the value of knowing these skills. These skills will take you a long way in a survival situation. Life can be pretty unpredictable; you never know where you're going to end up.

Start practicing these skills today; master them. The best thing about learning these skills is that you will not only be able to keep yourself alive, but you can also shoulder the burden of your loved ones. No one wants their children, parents, or siblings to suffer. This is a great chance for you to lead by example.

You do not have to master every skill mentioned above; you can pick out the skills you think are best for your survival. Also, you have now read several methods of performing the same task in this book. You can choose the method that you can execute best. Look around your area, note what kind of weather it usually has, and be aware of your resources. Only you can make the best decisions for yourself; this book is just to help you raise self-awareness. We cannot make your decisions for you, but we certainly can help you make the right decisions.